Same Same

Marthe Jocelyn • Tom Slaughter

Tundra Books

Published in Canada by Tundra Books,
75 Sherbourne Street, Toronto, Ontario M5A 2P9

Published in the United States by Tundra Books of Northern New York,
P.O. Box 1030, Plattsburgh, New York 12901

Library of Congress Control Number: 2008902721

Library and Archives Canada Cataloguing in Publication

Jocelyn, Marthe
        Same same / Marthe Jocelyn ; Tom Slaughter, illustrator.

Target audience: For ages 2-5.
ISBN 978-0-88776-885-9

        1. Set theory–Juvenile literature. I. Slaughter, Tom II. Title.

QA174.5.J62 2009   j511.3'2   C2008-901549-5

We acknowledge the financial support of the Government of Canada through the Book Publishing Industry Development Program (BPIDP) and that of the Government of Ontario through the Ontario Media Development Corporation's Ontario Book Initiative. We further acknowledge the support of the Canada Council for the Arts and the Ontario Arts Council for our publishing program.

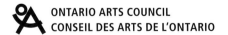 ONTARIO ARTS COUNCIL
CONSEIL DES ARTS DE L'ONTARIO

Medium: Painted paper cuts

Printed in China

1 2 3 4 5 6   14 13 12 11 10 09

For Hannah and Nell

round

things

things that

make music

things

that fly

striped
things

long things

things

that go

things in water

very big

things

things with

four legs

red

things . . .